The Ladybird Key Words Ea [...] these commonly used words. [...] the English language are introduced first — with other words of popular appeal to the learner. For example, the twelve most used words in English (a, and, he, I, in, is, it, of, that, the, to, was) which make up a quarter of all those the ordinary person reads and writes, are included in the 46 different words of Book 1.

Each book contains a list of the new words used. The gradual introduction of these words, frequent repetition and 'carry-over' from book to book, will ensure rapid learning.

The full-colour illustrations have been designed to create a desirable attitude towards learning, and to make the learner eager to read.

The information printed at the bottom of the coloured illustrations may be read aloud to the learner, to stimulate his interest further.

This series links with The Ladybird Key Words Reading Scheme. The author of both is W. Murray, an experienced headmaster, author and lecturer on the teaching of reading. W. Murray is co-author, with J. McNally, of 'Key Words to Literacy'—a teacher's book published by The Schoolmaster Publishing Co., Ltd., Derbyshire House, St. Chad's Street, London, W.C.1.

The Ladybird Key Words Easy Readers

Book One   The Record Breakers

Book Two   Danger Men

Book Three   A First 'Do You Know' Book

Book Four   A Second 'Do You Know' Book

Book Five   A Third 'Do You Know' Book

Book Six   Some Great Men and Women

(further titles in preparation)

These books are written on a controlled vocabulary and are graded in order of difficulty.

If the Teacher wishes, this series may be linked with the Ladybird Key Words Reading Scheme. Book One ("The Record Breakers") is about equal in reading difficulty to the third level of the Reading Scheme (i.e. Books 3a, 3b, 3c), Book Two ("Danger Men") with the fourth stage (4a, 4b, 4c) and so on.

Older non-readers may use these Ladybird Key Words Easy Readers as books for learning to read. Other children will also be attracted because of their interest and appeal.

A Ladybird Key Words Easy Reader

A SECOND
'Do You Know'
Book

by W. MURRAY
with illustrations by F. HUMPHRIS

Publishers: Ladybird Books Ltd . Loughborough
© Ladybird Books Ltd (formerly Wills & Hepworth Ltd) 1971
Printed in England

This is a picture of the sun, the earth, the moon and some planets in space.

The moon goes round the earth, and the earth goes round the sun. The planets all go round the sun.

Men can go to the moon. One day they may go to the planets.

new words   sun   earth
planets   round   may

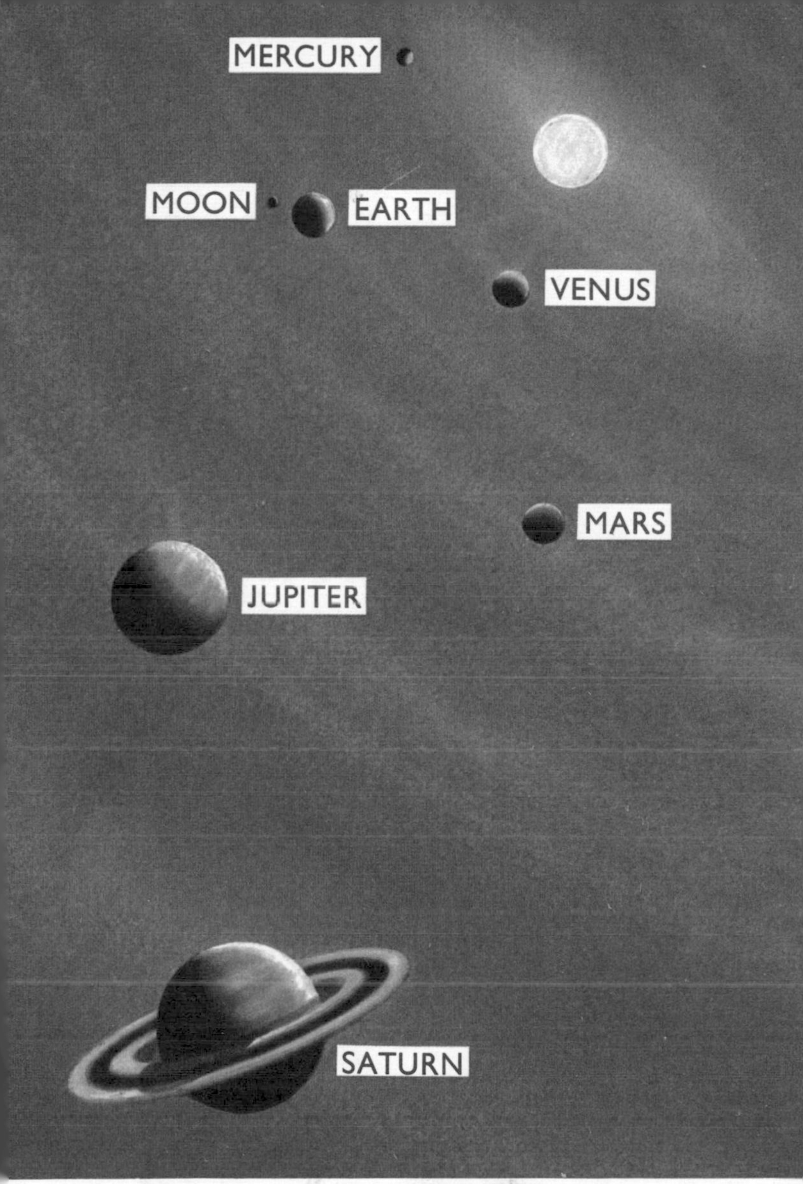

MERCURY

MOON ● EARTH

VENUS

MARS

JUPITER

SATURN

The earth is one of nine planets, all going round the sun, each at its own speed and in its own track. The picture shows the earth and some of these planets.

The man you see is by a large
meteorite. The meteorite looks
like rock, but has metal in it.
Meteorites come from space, and
they make holes in the earth
when they come down.

Many meteorites are small, some
are large and some are very
large. They all look like rock.

This one came down a long
time ago. It is one of the largest
meteorites.

new words   by   meteorite   rock
metal   when   came   ago

This is the largest meteorite that has landed during this century in the western world. It came down in the U.S.A. in the year 1902.

Here is a hole made by a meteorite when it came down to earth a very long time ago.

It is a large hole, made by a very large meteorite. How large is the hole?

We can see how large this hole is if we look at the bottom of it. When we do, we can see some buildings. As the hole is so large, the buildings look very small.

---

new words

made   How   we   if

This giant crater in the U.S.A. is nearly 3 miles (4·83 kms.) round. The tiny buildings at the bottom can hardly be seen. It is said that the crater was made long, long ago by a giant meteorite which exploded into dust.

Many miles down inside the
earth it is very hot. It is so hot
inside this planet that there is
no rock there. There is hot
lava. The lava looks like hot
mud. Hot lava can come from
a hole in the earth and make
a volcano.

A volcano is like a mountain with
a hole in the top. From inside
this hole in the top comes the
lava.

There are many mountains in the
world but not many volcanoes.

new words

inside   hot   lava   volcano

This is Mount Popocatepetl in Mexico.
There are about 450 active volcanoes in the world and there are thought
to be about 100 more under the sea.

There are very many kinds of living things in the sea. Some are very large, like the whale, and some are small. Some are so small that they have to be magnified for you to see them.

Here are some corals from the sea. Coral is something like rock, and is made by many, very small living things in the sea. It can grow to be very large.

Corals can be beautiful to look at.

---

new words

have   corals

Coral is made from the skeletons of hundreds of millions of tiny jelly-like creatures called coral polyps, which grow in the sea. A great many are beautifully coloured.
Those shown above are deep sea corals.

Do you know that an island can be made of coral? There are many coral islands. Some were made a long time ago.

These coral islands can be beautiful and they can be very large.

Coral islands can have grass, plants, flowers and trees on them. Men make buildings on some coral islands. Living on many of them are men, women, children, insects, birds and animals.

Coral grows only where the sun is hot.

new words

island   only

The Pacific Ocean has many coral islands and so has the Indian Ocean. They are also found in the West Indies and off the coasts of Florida and Brazil. The Bermuda group is a coral formation.

Very many kinds of fish live in the sea.

Some fish swim near the bottom of the sea. Others like to swim near the top. Some fish can jump from the water. There is one kind of fish that walks.

Here are some fish of many colours. The colours make them look beautiful.

There are many fish we like to eat. Some fish would hurt us if we were too near them in the sea.

new words

near   colours   would   us

HATCHET FISH

ANGEL FISH

PARROT FISH

SPOTTED
SCAT FISH

OL FISH

PARADISE FISH

Tropical fish, like the Angel, the Scat and the Idol, are brightly coloured. The Paradise fish can breathe air directly. The Parrot fish has teeth. The small Hatchet fish is one of the several kinds of flying fish.

All of us like to see a beautiful rainbow after we have had some rain. How many of us know how a rainbow is made?

Sunlight can be split into colours. The man in the first picture split sunlight into colours. You could do this.

After we have had rain, small drops of water in the air can split sunlight into colours to make a rainbow. We then look through the air and see these beautiful colours.

---

new words   rainbow   had   rain
sunlight   could   split   air

The scientist, Isaac Newton, placed a prism in the path of a sunbeam. He found that a sunbeam can be split into the colours of the rainbow.

A rainbow is produced by the action of sunlight on droplets of water in the air during and after rain.

In some storms we see lightning flash. Lightning comes from electricity in the air and the earth. In a storm like this, electricity in the air jumps to the earth to make a flash of lightning.

The flash of lightning in the air comes down something tall on the earth, like a tree or building.

The lightning could hurt us if we were under a tree in a storm like this.

---

new words

storms   lightning   flash   electricity

This shows lightning striking the Empire State Building in New York, America. No harm is done, as the electricity passes harmlessly down the lightning conductor on the building, into the earth.

This is a waterfall, a very large waterfall. It is one of the largest waterfalls in the world.

The water falls a long way at a great speed. There are drops of water in the air near the bottom of the waterfall, and when the sun is on these drops a rainbow is made.

The drops of water in the air split the sunlight into colours. The rainbow is beautiful to see.

new words

waterfall   great

Here are the famous Victoria Falls on the Zambesi river in Africa. When the sun shines on the water the spray forms a rainbow at the foot of the falls.

People must have water to live
and plants must have water
to grow.

When a dam is made, there is
water for many people and for
the things that grow in the earth.

People can boat on the water
of a dam and fish in it.

The waterfall made by a dam
can be used to make electricity.
Electricity has many uses, as
you know.

Some of the dams in the world
must be very large. Here is one
of the largest.

---

new words

people   must

This is the Kariba Dam, below the Victoria Falls on the Zambesi river. The dam supplies water and electricity. The man-made lake is 175 miles (281·66 kms.) long and 20 miles (32·19 kms.) wide.

These are pictures of some minerals. These minerals are not from the surface of the earth, we must get them from under the surface.

There are many kinds of minerals. Most of them are hard. Some are very hard, like diamonds, and may have beautiful colours. We have uses for most minerals.

There are minerals under the surface of the moon and some of these may be of use to us.

new words   minerals

surface   most   hard

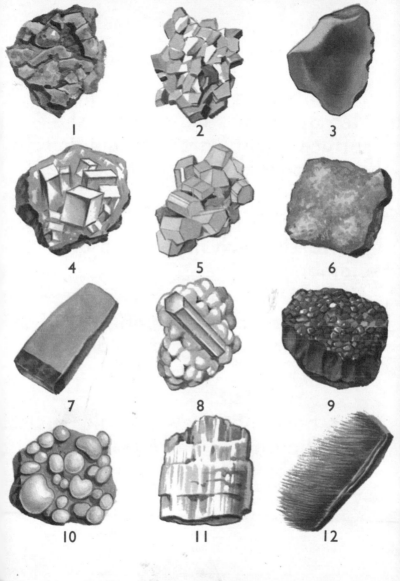

1 copper	2 silver	3 graphite or black-lead	4 rock salt
5 sulphur	6 gold	7 jade	8 emerald
9 ruby	10 turquoise	11 Epsom salts	12 asbestos

The ruby is a hard, red mineral. Men get rubies from under the surface of the earth. A ruby is split and cut to make it look beautiful.

Most people like rubies. A ruby may be worth much more than a diamond.

There are not very many rubies in the world, so they are worth much money.

Men now know how to make rubies. If we had many more rubies they would not be worth so much money.

---

new words   ruby   rubies   worth
much   more   money   now

A ruby is worth ten times as much as a diamond of the same weight.
The best rubies in the world have come from a valley in Upper Burma,
known as Moḡok. The picture shows this, with some of the ruby
diggings.

Long, long ago very large animals like these lived here on earth. There were many of them and they lived on this planet for a very long time. The ones you see in this picture were the largest of all.

There were no men living on the earth then, only animals, plants and fish.

There are no animals now like the ones in this picture. Only the blue whale is as big as they were then.

...ese were the biggest of the Dinosaurs which lived on earth millions of ...ars ago. They lived in swamps, because the water partly supported the ...ge weight of their bodies.

When you go into the sea you can sink. This man in the Dead Sea does not sink. He cannot sink. The Dead Sea has so much salt in it that the man cannot sink.

The Dead Sea has much more salt than other seas. Living things cannot live in it because there is so much salt.

Salt-water fish from other seas cannot live in this sea because of the salt.

It is very hot by the Dead Sea.

new words   sink   Dead
cannot   salt   because

The Dead Sea, by Jordan and Israel, is the lowest on the earth's surface.
The water contains more than 25 per cent of different kinds of salt.
There is no way out from the Dead Sea to other seas.

Many minerals are heavy. Metals are minerals, and they can be very heavy. There are many kinds of metals. Some are worth much more money than others because they are so useful.

Some metals are heavier than others. Iridium is a useful metal, and iridium is very heavy.

You can see that the large elephant in the picture is not as heavy as the iridium. The elephant is one of the largest and heaviest animals. Iridium is one of the heaviest metals.

---

new words	heavy	heavier	heaviest
	useful	iridium	elephant

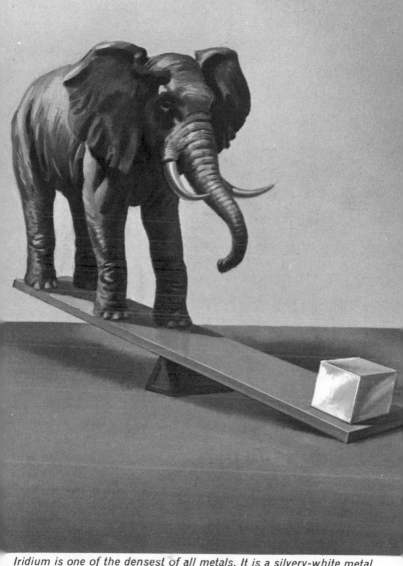

Iridium is one of the densest of all metals. It is a silvery-white metal of the platinum group and is very expensive. Quite a small cube would outweigh a large elephant. It is used for pen points and watch and compass bearings.

One of the most useful kinds of wood is teak. Teak wood is useful because it is strong, hard and heavier than most other woods. People like the look of teak and many things are made from it.

Teak trees grow only in countries where it is hot and wet. Elephants live in these countries where it is hot and wet. They help men to get the heavy wood to the water.

Elephants are big and strong, and they can do the heaviest work.

new words   teak   strong
           countries   where   wet

Teak is one of the most tough and weatherproof woods. Here you see teak logs being floated down a river. Teak is largely used for decks of ships, railway sleepers and indoor and outdoor furniture.

In countries of the world where it is wet and hot, some living things grow to be very large and strong.

This small boy lives where the hot sun makes the plants grow large.

The boy is on the water but he will not sink or get wet. He is on one of the very large, round leaves on the surface of the water.

If you were not very heavy, you could sit on the plant like this boy. You would not sink.

new words

boy   will

This little boy is Indian. He lives in Madras. He is sitting on the leaf of an enormous water-lily which floats on water.

Do you know of the Great Wall of China?

China is one of the great countries of the world. The Great Wall of China was made long ago. The wall was made to keep out the peoples of other countries, and it did keep them out.

The Great Wall is there now. If you go to China you will see it. The wall is very long and strong but it could not keep people out now. People can fly into China by aeroplane.

new words

Wall　China　keep　out

In the years 228 to 210 B.C. the Chinese built their Great Wall to keep out people who wanted to invade their country. The wall is 1,400 miles (2253·33 kms.) long.

Some parts of the world are hot, and some are cold. In parts where it is very cold there is ice on the sea.

The ice on the sea can be thick. It can be so thick that boats cannot go through it.

Here you can see thick ice on the sea. An ice-breaker is going through the ice, breaking it up. The ice-breaker is breaking a way for other boats.

new words   parts   cold
thick   ice-breaker   breaking

Ice-breakers break the winter ice of some rivers and seas to free a passage for shipping. These ships are very large and strongly made. Here is the S.S. Manhattan forcing her way through Arctic ice.

It is said that the dog is the animal people like most of all. Men, women and children like dogs. There are dogs in most parts of the world, in hot countries and in cold countries.

The tall girl is by a tall dog. This is said to be the tallest dog in the world.

The small girl is near a very small dog. This dog is said to be the smallest dog in the world. This girl is the smallest of the three girls in the picture.

new words

said   girl   smallest

The world's tallest breed of dog is the Irish Wolfhound. The record height is 39½ inches (1·00 m.) at the shoulders.
The smallest breed of dog in the world is the Chihuahua. It comes from Mexico. The smallest one weighs only 2 pounds (0·908 kgms.).

Look at the legs and tail of this kangaroo. The legs and tail are large and strong.

The kangaroo uses its strong legs and tail to jump a very long way.

It can jump higher than all other animals. It can jump higher than an elephant is tall.

Do you see that the kangaroo has a pouch? Inside its pouch it keeps the baby kangaroo. It can jump with the baby kangaroo in its pouch.

This animal eats grass and the leaves of trees.

---

new words   legs   tail   kangaroo
its   pouch   baby

Kangaroos are found in Australia. The greatest known height jumped by a kangaroo is 10' 6" (3.2 m.). The longest known jump is 42 feet (12.8 m.). The red kangaroo has reached speeds of 45 m.p.h. (72.42 kms.).

Here is a man who lifts weights.
Look at him, he is big and strong.
He can lift more than you and I.
He can lift heavier weights than
most other men.

The man is a weight-lifter. He
lifts weights to see how strong
he is. People come to see him.
They like to see him lift heavier
and heavier weights.

They see him with weight-lifters
from other countries. They like
to see who will lift the heaviest
weights.

new words

lifts   weights   him   weight-lifter

Weight-lifters compete according to their own weights.
They compete under three headings:— Press, Snatch and Jerk, and then
add the three weights lifted. A world record lift of 1,300½ lbs.
(590·0 kgms.) was made by a Russian in 1967.

Can you read the words when you cover the pictures?

(1) Here are the sun, earth and moon.

(2) Meteorites come from space.

(3) Hot lava comes from a volcano.

(4) Some islands are made of coral.

(5) Drops of water split sunlight into colours.

(6) Lightning is electricity in the air.

(7) A waterfall can be beautiful.

(8) Many minerals are useful.

(9) A ruby is worth much money.

(10) The man cannot sink in the Dead Sea.

(11) Teak trees are tall and strong.

(12) Here is the Great Wall of China.

(13) Iridium is one of the heaviest metals

(14) An ice-breaker can break thick ice.

(15) Most boys and girls like dogs.

(16) The kangaroo has a baby in its pouch.

(17) Weight-lifters can lift heavy weights.

no new words

Words new to the series used in this book

Page

4 sun earth planets round may

6 by meteorite rock metal when came ago

8 made How we if

10 inside hot lava volcano

12 have corals

14 island only

16 near colours would us

18 rainbow had rain sunlight could split air

20 storms lightning flash electricity

22 waterfall great

24 people must

26 minerals surface most hard

28 ruby rubies worth much more money now

Page

30 —

32 sink Dead cannot salt because

34 heavy heavier heaviest useful iridium elephant

36 teak strong countries where wet

38 boy will

40 Wall China keep out

42 parts cold thick ice-breaker breaking

44 said girl smallest

46 legs tail kangaroo its pouch baby

48 lifts weights him weight-lifter

50 —

Total number of new words used - 94